AN

ADDRESS

DELIVERED BEFORE THE

BOSTON YOUNG MEN'S CHRISTIAN ASSOCIATION,

ON THE OCCASION OF THEIR FIRST ANNIVERSARY, IN PARK STREET CHURCH, BOSTON, TUESDAY EVENING, MAY 25, 1852.

BY CHAS. THEO. RUSSELL.

PUBLISHED BY REQUEST OF THE SOCIETY.

GEO. C. RAND,
PRINTER, NO. 3 CORNHILL, BOSTON.
1852.

AN

ADDRESS

DELIVERED BEFORE THE

BOSTON YOUNG MEN'S

CHRISTIAN ASSOCIATION,

ON THE OCCASION OF THEIR FIRST ANNIVERSARY, IN PARK STREET CHURCH, BOSTON, TUESDAY EVENING, MAY 25, 1852.

By CHAS. THEO. RUSSELL.

PUBLISHED BY REQUEST OF THE SOCIETY.

GEO. C RAND,
PRINTER, NO. 3 CORNHILL, BOSTON
1852.

Boston, May 26th, 1852.

HON. CHAS. THEO. RUSSELL, Boston.

DEAR SIR:—It is my privilege to communicate below a vote passed at the conclusion of the public services before the Boston Young Men's Christian Association, held last evening in Park Street Church:—

"Voted, that the thanks of this Association be presented to Hon. Charles Theodore Russell, for the able and eloquent address delivered before them this evening, and that the Secretary be instructed to request a copy for publication."

Your Obedient Servant,

JAMES W. MERRIAM, *Rec. Secretary.*

Boston, May 29th, 1852.

JAMES W. MERRIAM, ESQ.,

Rec. Sec'y B. Y. Men's Ch. Association.

DEAR SIR:— I received your letter of the 26th instant, communicating to me the vote of the Boston Young Men's Christian Association, requesting a copy of my address before them, on Tuesday evening last, for publication. I am deeply sensible of the kindness with which the Association received this address, and which I am afraid renders their judgment too partial. The address was written in the hurried intervals, snatched from legislative and professional engagements; and I did not suppose it would deserve the permanent preservation of the press. As, however, the Society have thought otherwise, and as the address may possibly make known, to some extent, the objects and necessities of the institution, I submit my judgment to theirs, and the manuscript to their disposal.

With my best wishes for the prosperity of this noble Association, and with many thanks for the kind expression of their vote, and to you personally for the manner you have communicated it, I am,

Very respectfully,

Your Obedient Servant,

CHAS. THEO. RUSSELL.

ADDRESS.

Introducing to the multitude that crowds our anniversary week another claimant for the sympathy and support of our religious community, we neither expect nor desire its unchallenged reception to the hallowed fireside, where we would establish it. Seeking a place among the recognized auxiliaries of the church, we solicit a position of Christian confidence and love; and, before it is granted, we anticipate, and it is fitting we should meet, a scrutiny proportioned to the relation sought. We come to a circle, guarded with ceaseless and appropriate vigilance, abounding in love, but equally in objects to share it. When we ask to open and extend the sacred enclosure, to a new, although not strange comer, we should be prepared to vindicate a claim to the honor desired.

Emerging into life, when a multiplicity of associations confuses the action and divides the energies of the benevolent, we must present more than a society, professing Christian purposes, and striving for useful ends, to secure permanent establishment in the community. There must be some special want, deeply felt, which we meet,—some object of reasonable importance, which we accomplish. In moral, as in ordinary machinery, every wheel imposed upon the motive power, however symmetrical in form, or beautiful in motion, is only a burden, if it serve no special purpose, and add nothing to the final product. In moral, as in ordinary machinery, too, our effort should be to simplify and thus reduce to a minimum friction and complication. To create, therefore, an association to do what kindred institutions are already doing, or what individuals may well accomplish, is worse than useless. Nor is it sufficient that the mode is improved. It must be an improvement fairly proportioned to the trouble and cost incurred.

With all this admitted, we must still remember that the motive power may exist for ages, unfelt and unproductive, because no appropriate machinery directs it to the working point. The waters leaped and plunged for centuries, in grandeur and sublimity only, till human invention conducted their accumulated and diffused power, by wheel, shaft, and loom, to the point which throws the fabric off. The vapor, in whose expansive force slumbered the destiny of nations, rose, fell, and rose again, from the beginning of time, till the genius of man brought it to toil and spin — to speed the ship across the ocean, and the iron courser along the land. The silent power, which, as the messenger of civilization, distances the hours, and outstrips the chariot of the sun, lay dormant where God placed it, till exact appliances made it instinct with life and intelligence. The limpid waters of the lake repose in tranquil beauty, but neither refresh nor invigorate, till the proper conduits bring them to the thirsty people. "The pure river of water of life, clear as chrystal, proceeding out of the throne of God and of the Lamb," and of which he that drinketh shall never thirst, must be brought, uncontaminated, through the polluted and defiling streams, which flow between it and them, to the parched lips of the expiring soul. Wheresoever a new channel can be opened to this life-giving fountain, there is a field for new laborers; and whosoever appropriately enters it will be cheered by the smile, and received to the fellowship, of all who serve the same Master. Encouraged by these considerations, we have organized our association. Various denominations, in a spirit of Christian love, have united to give it being, and to watch and guard its young life. Baptist clergymen, Methodist divines, reverend bishops, and the straitest ministry of Congregationalism have gathered to its consecration. All conceded it a fit subject for baptism, and none cared how the rite was performed, so that it was immersed in holy love, and sprinkled by the Divine Spirit. Upon its infant forehead churchmen have impressed the sacred sign of the cross, and the very elect of Puritanism have prayed that the impression be indelible.

Gratifying as is this fraternal spirit, and strongly as its concurrence marks the necessity of an institution like ours, there still comes the practical and searching enquiry, why are ye, what do you propose, and how will you accomplish it? As your organ, Mr. President, and gentlemen, you direct me this evening to answer, to the kind friends who meet us here, this enquiry.

The Boston Young Men's Christian Association was organized on the 22d of December last, and its purpose, in the brief language of its constitution, is "the improvement of the spiritual and mental condition of young men." In accomplishing this grand and general object, it neither supercedes nor interferes with any existing agency. It gratefully recognizes the church as its parent. It ranges itself in harmony and co-operation with subordinate institutions, which have risen about us responsive to the command, "beginning at Jerusalem," to "preach the gospel to every creature." Not sectarian, it is yet highly religious in its aims. It occupies a void no other society has sought, and no individual effort is adequate to fill. Local in name, it is wide and diffusive in purpose. An institution of young men, to-night and always, it solicits the counsel and support of those whose riper experience and more mature judgment can best guide it to success. Christian in title, it uses that term in its broad and catholic sense. It encourages the cultivation of literature, science and art, but all for the education of the immortal spirit. In the night, which ever surrounds us, sometimes bright and imposing, but often dark and cheerless; amid all the stars of the firmament, it follows only the guidance of that sweet and radiant light which, rejoicing the wise men of the East, went before them, till it "stood over where the young child was." It lays no injunction upon the fountains of learning or philosophy, but it would mingle with all their streams the purifying waters from

——"Siloa's brook, that flow'd
Fast by the oracle of God."——

It aspires to develope the intellectual nature, but under a well-regulated and active conscience, guided by the truths of divine revelation. Its distinguishing characteristic is the prominence it gives the strictly religious element, and the mode it adopts to bring the intellect and social feelings to its support. It is thus it meets a want long felt, and in which it has its existence.

Of Christian churches, where the gospel is preached, and the ordinances of religion from Sabbath to Sabbath administered, our Puritan city, from its foundation, has had a goodly share. These, with the enlightened ministry they sustain, after the revelation of God, are the bulwarks of our religion, and the grand conservators of our social and political institutions. Deriving their origin and authority from the Scriptures, they can neither resign, nor be deprived of, their first place in the Christian economy.

Nor has our city any lack of benevolent or missionary associations, directing themselves to the moral and physical improvement of the poor, the suffering, and the guilty. Charitable societies for mutual, general, or limited relief, meet us, in multiplied forms, in all directions. Temperance has its self-denying advocates, and its numerous and affiliated organizations. The benevolence of our community has wrought out varied channels, and filled them with its gushing waters.

Nor have we any want of mere literary associations. Besides those of more restricted and elevated character, which have so long distinguished our metropolis, there are others of a popular description, deriving their support and energy from the young men, and equally honorable to their originators as useful to their members. The ardor, the intelligence, the sagacious ambition of these young men have surrounded us with societies, bearing their impress and superscription. Some are general; some devoted to particular classes. The mechanics' apprentices have theirs. While the merchants' clerks, sustained by the generous countenance of the merchants themselves, by well-directed efforts and judicious management, have established an institution as honorable to the reputation of our city abroad, as essential to its prosperity at home. The munificence of a single individual has left little to be desired in the way of public lectures, within the scope of his noble bequests. Commerce, and the necessities of material interests, have originated and sustain various reading rooms. Libraries of large extent and liberal regulations are about us. No man for a moment doubts the beneficent results of these educational institutions, or supposes that they can be essentially improved in what they assume to do.

Our Society has an ultimate and direct purpose distinct from all these. It seeks not the duties or responsibilities of the church. It is not a charitable institution, nor library, nor literary association. It is a Christian Union, combining lecture, library, reading room, and social meeting for the direct "promotion of evangelical religion," among two classes,—the young men already in the city, and those daily coming to it.

For this end it has been organized; to this purpose dedicated. To preserve it true to its infant and public consecration, its management, by its constitution, is devolved upon those only who are members of some one of the churches of the four denominations composing it. This restriction extends to its management, and not to its privileges. Any person of good moral character may participate in the latter, but only church members control the former.

We have imposed this restriction in no spirit of sectarianism. I have already said the controlling purpose of this Association is the advancement of evangelical truth, by which I mean the great truths embodied in the common belief of the denominations here united. I do not stop to discuss the importance of these truths, or how far they are essential to human salvation, and the best interests of man. It is enough that we believe them so. Others may think us mistaken. Our belief must guide our action. With such an object our Society is as comprehensive as it can be. To make it more so we must abandon its distinctive character; or, disguising it, secure a support neither justice nor frankness will sanction.

Thus explicitly avowing our ends, and framing our Association to accomplish them, we do so in the spirit of Christian charity. So far as we traverse common ground we shall rejoice to go along in harmony and sympathy with kindred associations. Where our paths diverge, we shall part, I trust, with mutual respect, and pleasant remembrances, each wishing the other a prosperous journey. We embark upon a common sea, but with somewhat different objects, and seeking divergent points. It is not, therefore, for the comfort of either that we should embark together; but, upon so much of the ocean track as we pursue in company, we shall have no collision, but each to the other give the friendly hail and the manly cheer. If others select an anchorage we deem not safe, and we, in the exercise of the right we concede, choose another, our moorings and barks must be separate, but we shall part with no less respect because each acts upon his own conscience and judgment.

By the terms of our constitution, " any young man, who is a member in regular standing of an evangelical church, may become an active member of the Association by the payment of one dollar annually. Such members only have the right to vote, and are eligible to office. Any young man of good moral character, by the payment of a like sum, becomes a member, entitled to all other privileges. Life membership, subject to the same distinction, is created by the payment of twenty dollars."

The immediate management of the Society is devolved upon a board of officers, consisting of a President, four Vice Presidents, two Secretaries, a Treasurer, and Librarian; and a Standing Committee of two from each evangelical church in the city. That a proper efficiency may co-exist with an organization thus diffusive, this committee choose annually twelve of their number, who, with the officers named, constitute the board of managers.

This, in brief, is our organization. It originated, in the language of our constitution, from a "strong desire for the promotion of evangelical religion among the young men of our city, and an impression of the importance of concentrated effort for our own spiritual welfare, and that of those from without who may be brought under our influence."

Its object is distinctly written upon its front. It proposes to accomplish it, in the first place, by bringing into active sympathy and co-operation all who unite in desiring it. It recognizes the power of Christian union, and gratefully throws itself upon those auspicious tendencies of our time, which, in spirit (like the descending hosts upon the plains of Judea) proclaim, "Glory to God in the highest, and on earth peace, good will to men!" Seizing, not upon denominational agreement, but that love which Christ made the test of discipleship, it entrenches itself in united hearts, concurring hands, and common prayers. Seeking never to disturb the cherished associations, or distinguishing views of those who worship in this mountain, or at Jerusalem, but rising heaven-ward in spirit and truth, it aspires to draw thence a sacred fire to kindle a holier and brighter flame on all these altars. It regards denominations, as it has been said the sun looks down upon the great ocean, thence to drink up all that is sweet and invigorating, while it leaves all that is salt and bitter behind. And yet, what is left is not the less important in its place, because pernicious if taken from it. In the salt sea, with ceaseless tides and tumultuous agitations, earth finds its replenishing reservoirs. Under the genial sun, lifting the showers from their ocean bed, reviving nature spreads her lovely verdure at our feet.

Protestantism, it is sometimes said, is united only as a negation, and has no unities as a positive system. Various sects, it is asserted, divide it, unsympathizing, if not hostile, and each adhering with the tenacity of conscientious conviction of their truth and importance, to their distinguishing views. Says Lord Bacon, "they be two things—unity and uniformity." So far as the deadening and crushing influence of the latter is a power or a blessing, Protestantism has it not. But associations, like those of the week that is upon us, reveal in it a unity, rising in stately grandeur from the foundations of a common faith, and gathering strength and beauty from the diversities under which that faith is manifested. Protestantism is no broad and stagnant empire, but a union of independent communities, each jealous of the liberty wherewith Christ hath made it free. It has its separate states, with distinct and well-guarded boundaries, where conscience, private judgment, taste, feeling, — prejudice even, have their scope and embodiment. It has too its union, reposing upon the voluntary grants of the constituent, and over which no representative eagle, but the soft-pinioned dove, soars, bearing in her gentle beak the "*E Pluribus Unum*" of Christian love, and on her life-giving wings the healing of the nations. This is the unity of Protestantism, instinct with life, and deriving its being and power from that free spirit which, first originating denominations, has welled up in perpetual and energetic activity from them. Before it, fully developed, the hosts of infidelity, superstition, and sin, will not question its existence or might.

Something of this unity, our society, in its humble sphere, developes, but rather incidentally than as an ultimate end. It is not an alliance for the sake of union, but a union for the promotion of definite objects. These I have stated, and now proceed to what it has done, and proposes to do, to accomplish them.

Enabled by a liberal and gratifying support from our

immediate community, we have opened at a conspicuous and convenient point in the city, a large hall for the triple purpose of a reading, library, and social room. Attractive in character and appearance, supplied with the current journals and periodicals, and possessing what shall be the foundation of a Christian library, it is the resort of numbers of our young men for mutual acquaintance, conversation, social intercourse, information, and improvement. It is a kind of religious exchange, where men meet, not to discuss the rise and fall of property, the change of markets, or the ever-varying interests of trade, but to share each other's joys and sorrows, to speak of one faith and destiny, to indulge the out-gushings of a common sympathy, and to dwell amid the pauses of business life upon those great themes which make the heart burn within us. Here heart responds to heart, hand opens to hand, and "the threefold cord" is woven "which is not quickly broken." The young, ardent, and hopeful of our churches are here brought into communion and concert, and their souls strengthened by mutual counsel and encouragement. Under such inspiring influence, how is the heart refreshed, the mind elevated, and the arm nerved! How drinks in the soul the new sympathies which surround it, and thence gathering strength, soar in bolder flights to the clear heaven above! What courage hence drawn for sterner conflicts with sin and Satan! From these commingling streams an accumulated current will flow, in its onward course sweeping away some, at least, of the corruptions which endanger the moral health of our city.

But not alone upon church members does our Association act. In addition to what I have stated, it contemplates courses of formal and elaborate, as well as familiar and social, lectures. It thus proposes and hopes, by reading room, library, lecture, and social intercourse, to draw members within its influence, and away from places of idle and pernicious amusement. Thus, by the blessing of Divine Providence, it trusts to lead many among us, "in the days of their youth, to remember their creator, God," and having learned "the beginning of wisdom," to walk ever in her "ways of pleasantness," and her "paths of peace." We desire to avail ourselves, for religious purposes, of that social feeling which seeks gratification in the club or reunion, and to open, amid the temptations of a great city, a place of resort and culture, pervaded by an atmosphere of religious truth and the influences of the Christian fireside.

Our Society has one other object quite as characteristic and important as any I have named. All who hear me know how great a proportion of our city comes from the surrounding country. A glance at the list of those in public stations, or a catalogue of our merchants or mechanics, shows how large a part are not native born. The sad and mournful records of our prisons are no exception. The terrible but unrevealed lists of the votaries of intemperance, licentiousness, vice, and sin, will alone develope, in ghastly greatness, the living hecatombs New England here pours into a sea of moral death. They come joyous and bright as the streams that dance and sparkle in the morning sun upon her mountain sides. The cottage sends them forth its richest treasure, and with them its purest love and proudest hope. They have shared the sweet influences of many a "cotter's Saturday night," and are fresh from scenes like those whence

> "Old Scotia's grandeur springs,
> That makes her loved at home, revered abroad."

Morning and evening they have kneeled at the fireside altar, and around them float the breathings of parental prayer, soft as strains of gentle music. They come from happy family circles, which their departure ruptures, and the twining tendrils they have unbound stretch forth for kindred support. No sympathetic circle expands for their reception. No domestic fireside invites to its hallowed precincts. No familiar church opens its door. No long-recognized voice solicits to the house of prayer. On every side are beating hearts, and living forms, but amid all, they are strangers and alone. Their relations are those of business; and when, this ended, the silent and sacred hours (heretofore the sweetest of life) approach, the heart aches with its dreary solitude. Who has not felt the desolation of such a moment, when a single word of sympathy falls upon the sternest heart, as the prophet's rod touched the rock, and drew forth its gushing waters?

This is not more the Christian's than the tempter's hour, and Satan will besiege the ear, till ministering angels drive him thence. Then the mind discriminates least, and any voice that says, "Come with me and I will do thee good," finds a responsive listener. The monitions of conscience yield to the soft pleadings of the heart. The social nature imperiously craves sustenance, and too often, like the starving prodigal, would fain fill itself with the very husks upon which the swine feed.

All do not fall in such an hour. Thanks be to heaven there is no trial without its support, as there is no Gethsemane without its angel! Many come forth unscathed — but always to mingle with the thanksgiving of victory the more earnest prayer against temptation. Others have no such thanksgiving to offer. How many a fondly-loved son, in an hour like this, with a mother's parting tear wet on his cheek, has encountered a friendship sincere but fatal, which has led him from one scene of amusement and dissipation to another, till the ocean of life has cast him a mutilated wreck at his parents' feet! How many a mother, beside such a wreck, in an anguish desolating as the sorrows of death drew from Israel's king, has cried, "O my son Absalom, my son, my son, Absalom — would God I had died for thee, O Absalom, my son, my son!" How many a sister has clasped to her heart such a brother, returning with the prodigal's fate, but not his penitence, and poured upon his shame-stricken cheeks tears bitter as those of

Mary at the grave of Lazarus, while she has relieved the bursting agonies of her soul (in the language of Martha's faith) "I know, that even now whatsoever thou shalt ask of God, God will give it thee!" How many a father has seen the pride of his manhood, the disgrace of his later years, planting a thorn in the dying pillow of pious age!

No scheme devised can remedy all these harrowing evils. Our Society proposes to do something to mitigate them, by surrounding young men, when the temptations and trials of city life begin, with proper influences, aid, and counsel.

To accomplish this it has opened a communication with the pastor of every evangelical church in New England. It designs thus to be brought into acquaintance with the young men, who yearly and daily leave their homes, to mingle in and make the swelling aggregate of our city's prosperity and population. Thus introduced, we propose to meet them at their entrance, and in the hours I have described, and at all times, to furnish some substitute for the kindly sympathies and affectionate circle they have left. We purpose to aid them in finding a home at some fireside where the altar of God has a place, and, consulting their views and feelings, lead them to the church of their choice, and leave them in its faithful watch and ward. Connected by correspondence with the religious societies of the country, and by organization with those of the city, it is our aim to see that none fall by, or linger too long on, the way between the two. By the social intercourse, congenial feeling, and interest of our rooms, we hope to dispel the homesick loneliness of a first entrance upon the wide world, and seizing upon that impressible hour, to bind the affections indissolubly to us. Confidence is to be secured by counsel and sympathy; the friendships of youth formed by individual taste and judgment, but in an atmosphere of Christian feeling.

It is this feature which invests our society with a far other than local interest, and fixes upon it the regard and affection of multitudes, who never themselves coming within the sphere of its action, will bless its kindly influences over those most dear. If it succeeds in this feature, it will have done enough to secure the love and support of a rural community, contributing hourly to the growth of our metropolis, with trembling anxiety, the very jewels of its heart. If we are faithful here, not more certainly will the curling smoke ascend from the hill-sides and valleys of New England, to greet the morning sun, than the prayers of an earnest faith for a blessing upon our labors. Our Association will become an object of affection in the family, where many a son and brother, cheered by its smile, and led by its influence to "the still waters" and "green pastures," will make its name no unfamiliar sound. Not only shall we have the prayers of fathers and mothers, but may we not hope the little ones even of the fireside will sometimes bear us up to "Jesus, tender shepherd," as

> "they lay them down to sleep,
> And pray the Lord their soul to keep."

And certain as the revelation of God, has that great Shepherd declared that whosoever taketh in, when a stranger, the least of his brethren, hath done the goodly deed to *him*.

Such is our institution; such its organization; and briefly, some of its objects. In its origin it has sought the counsels of the aged and wise; in its management it throws itself upon the young and active. A medium between the churches of city and country, it claims the support of both. Seeking the good of the young, it demands their co-operation and vigorous effort. It presents itself not as a charity, but as a necessity and attraction. It desires to live not upon the sense of duty, but upon love and interest. It sees science, commerce, trades, special interests, with large and flourishing associations, and it fearlessly asks if these be stronger bonds of union, or surer guaranties of life, than a common Christian faith. It looks upon social clubs on every hand, sustained by refined intelligence and large expense, and it boldly hazards the experiment of such an institution, founded on the deep sympathies of religion, and hearts swayed by one transcendent motive.

So far as the experiment has gone it has met our most sanguine expectations. Our Association was formed on the 22d of December, adopted its constitution on the 29th of the same month, and elected its first board of officers on the 5th of January following. It has a large and increasing catalogue of annual and life members. It has received from these liberal contributions. It has obtained an act of incorporation, and organized under it. As I have already stated, it has opened convenient and attractive rooms, and supplied them with the journals and periodicals of the day. It has commenced a library, and by the donations of various publishing societies and a few generous individuals, has upon its shelves several hundred volumes. It has established a communication with the pastors of New England. It is fully launched upon its active duties. The young men of our churches send it forth in hope and joy. They have invoked upon it the spirit and blessing of God, and pledged it the support of manly hands and generous hearts. To-night, here assembled, they present it, to you their honored and reverend seniors, and ask you to receive it among the cherished institutions which on this sacred week keep holy time in our Jerusalem. They seek not your charity, but your influence and approbation. Young men, they can never want the sweet sympathies stirred by the remembrance that to you once

> "Life itself was new,
> And the heart promised what the fancy drew."

They solicit your counsels and efforts to rear upon the foundations they have laid in faith and confidence, Jesus Christ being the chief corner-stone, a structure where your sons shall find a defence against the assaults of temptation and sin, and within which they shall "both hope, and quietly wait for the salvation of the Lord."

Gentlemen of the Association, you have planted this,

it may be, the smallest of seeds. You have watched and watered it. By the power of him "who giveth the increase" you look for a goodly tree, whose fruits shall be healing and its leaves peace. May it spring up, and thousands reposing therein bless its grateful shade! While "dwelling together in unity" about it, your hearts shall distil upon leaf, and branch, and root, influences sweet "as the dew of Hermon, and as the dew that descended upon the mountains of Zion, for there the Lord commanded the blessing, even life for ever more."

www.ingramcontent.com/pod-product-compliance
Lightning Source LLC
LaVergne TN
LVHW011140110826
845150LV00008B/2436
9781418193294